The Beasts & the Elders

The University Press of
New England

SPONSORING INSTITUTIONS
Brandeis University
Clark University
Dartmouth College
University of New Hampshire
University of Rhode Island
University of Vermont

The Beasts  the Elders

by Robert Siegel

Published for Dartmouth College by

The University Press of New England

Hanover, New Hampshire 1973

2/1974
am. Lit

Library of Congress Catalogue Card number: 73-77481
ISBN 0-87451-080-5 Clothbound
ISBN 0-87451-085-6 Paperbound

Printed in the United States of America

The author is grateful to the following publications for assignment of copyrights and permission to reprint: "The Rock," winner of the 1970 Foley Award, copyright 1970 by America Press, Inc.; *The Atlantic Monthly:* "Air Field," formerly "Hanscom Air Field"; *Boston University Journal:* "The Catch," "Turnpike: Exit 144," "Laodicea, New Hampshire," "Love Story: The Sixties"; *Chicago Tribune Magazine:* "Gettysburg: The Wheatfield," "The Cow"; *The Georgia Review:* "Grandfather Chance"; *Granite:* "At the Edge," "The Hunt," "Hunting in Widener Library," "Leaves of Grass: 1860," "March Moon," "The Moose on Ledyard Bridge," "Poet," "Voice of Many Waters"; *Poetry:* "A Bear," "Ego," "A Visit to the Farm," copyright 1971, 1972 by the Modern Poetry Association; *Poetry Northwest:* "The Shot," "The Journey"; *Prairie Schooner:* "In a Farmhouse Near Porlock"; *The Quest* (now *The Little Magazine*): "Mad Dog"; *Sightseers Into Pilgrims:* "Snakesong," copyright 1973 by Tyndale House Publishers.

To My Mother & Father
And Roberta

Contents

Foreword

Robert Siegel's poems show a wide range of feelings and are lighted with brilliant intellectual perceptions under sensitive controls of form, rhythm, and diction. His poems tend to be objective, sometimes thick in make, but there is a great deal of subjective feeling behind them. They have a strange new tensile strength, a kind of rigorous thrusts at truth, and some have an airy and dream-like quality. He has a sense of world-animation, and you can feel him trying to pin down manifold and various feelings, perceptions, and attitudes to produce the right blend of meaning and suggestion. Or at least I can. I have seen him able to change lines at will and have admired his ability to change words or passages until they are finally as he wants them.

Siegel is very much his own man. He can be narrative, anecdotal, or lyrical by turns, as those poems drawn from the Civil War demonstrate. He has a fine grasp not only of situations and things but of persons and their relationships.

These poems are strongly intellectual. They contend physically, or as if physically, with a real world and give off a this-worldly quality rather than being primarily of a metaphysical stamp. Yet if I were writing some time ago of this new poet and his first book, I would say that he has something of Donne in him. But Donne is not a touchstone in the seventies and I use his name only to suggest that Robert Siegel makes a complex kind of intellectual poetry of strong linguistic grain and carefully wrought forms.

One of the best things to say about a new poet is whether one wishes to read his poems again, or often. I keep reading Siegel's.

These poems give me real pleasure. They have a reality of their own, a ruggedness and prescience confronting life direct-ly. Robert Siegel's poems invite participation. It is a pleasure to get his drift and feel his brunt.

Richard Eberhart

I saw four and twenty elders sitting,
clothed in white raiment;
and they had on their heads crowns of gold. . . .
And round about the throne,
were four beasts . . . full of eyes within:
and they rest not day and night, saying,
Holy, holy, holy, Lord God Almighty,
which was, and is, and is to come.
And when those beasts give glory . . .
the four and twenty elders fall . . .
and cast their crowns before the throne.

Revelation 4:4–10

One

Ego   has thrust his nose under every board,
smelt out every wild carrot and white grub,
stucco'd the dirt with his tracks from side
to side, rubbed smooth the corner
posts, left his pink, red-bristled hide
on every barb of five strands of wire;

chewed the bark from the one scrub pine
that pitches a ghost of shade at noon,
bangs incessantly the metal trough-lid
at off-hours, chuffs down the white meal
raising a cloud around his ears, and cleans
each cob with the nicety of a Pharisee

tooth for tooth, squeezing contentedly
his small bagpipe voice as he mashes
corn with a slobbery leer and leaves
turds like cannonballs across a battlefield.
Meanwhile his little pink eye is
periscoped on the main chance—

the gate ajar, the slipped board,
the stray ducky that flusters through the wire—
saliva hanging from his mouth like a crown jewel.
His jowels shake with mirth under the smile
that made a killing on the market, won the fifth
    caucus,
took the city against all odds.

No wonder we shake at the thought of his getting out
of his square patch, electrify the wire,
(At night we hear him thump his dreams
on the corrugated tin hut and shudder,

1

the single naked bulb in there burning
through our sleep like his eye!),

take special dietary precautions against
his perpetual rut, except that March day
we drag the yearling sow to him
through mud up to his hocks. From that handseling
comes the fat litter—the white one for the Fair,
the spotted black to be slaughtered in November.

We don't show him to the neighbors, though in June,
framed by clover and bees stringing out the sun, he is
quite grand, an enormous blimp supporting
intelligent waggish ears, regally lidded eyes and
a pink glistening snout
ready to shove up the privates of the world.

The Shot

for
David Perkins

*"Why look'st thou so?"—With my cross-bow
I shot the Albatross.*

If he could have taken ship again,
watched the cobalt veins of the white clouds,
the sliding wrinkle of the planet's skin
come ever on, swung at the mainmast's tip
like a bell on the ringing waves, and watched
the seabirds spiral down as in a well—

if he could have, he would not, of course:
all that glanced over in a line or two,
weeks of good weather worth no comment,
unless that on the edge of days shaped
perfectly as a bubble a slight mist
teased the corner of one eye. Looking back

it was the good days he resented most—
the sun rising on the left like a carpenter's plumb,
sinking on the right as the captain walked the deck
puffing at every third step on his pipe.

Then the storm came. How well he remembered
his nerves crawling with lightning along the ropes:
no time to think, the deck usually a wall,
the air foul in the hold where he huddled
tingling with rope-burns, almost glad,
against backs shivering and wet as his own.

Now the cold, and the floating ice
misshapen as his thoughts. Majestic, strange,
the enormous bird—still as iced sails
big with moon or landing and cavernously
shrugging off the world, its eye upon him.

3

Daily it made a dizzy play catching
food in the air or coming among the silly crew
with hubbub of wings. It drew the moment out
gliding in narrow circles about the ship.
He never could recall just when he shot.

A Visit to the Farm

Whoever colored the moon tonight didn't stay
within the lines—it melts across the sky.
Each leaf thrusts close its breath and frogs
white in the headlights' tunnel eye
flirt with death on quick parabolas.

At Uncle Joe's the television screen
aimed its blue dance across our faces
while a hen chuckled sleepily over an egg
deep in impenetrable darkness.
Whining, the dog dropped softly on the porch

an unweened rabbit no bigger than a mouse.
As we lingered by the car, the windmill light
burned a naked period in the dark
over a tractor comatose upon its haunches.
Cats ghosted and gleamed in the barn's murk

or wrapped their backs about our legs
pleading with small murderous motors.
Now down miles of vanished road the light
sinks to a hardly noticeable star.
The moon lifts over fog and dashlights

show precise green teeth under a wide eye.
I stretch, glad to have escaped the city
muffled in the distance of this plain
toward which TV towers wink with small red eyes,
each leading its oafish fellow on a chain.

State Hospital

On the dirty brick walls the late sun
smoulders to rose. Behind black panes of glass
children stare straight through the woodwork
signed by passing hands. Someone bangs
repeatedly an iron railing,

a syncopated bell announcing
the unreal hour that fills all the buildings
to the black chimney brim,
whose eye stretches behind all these windows
that never open or fall asleep.

In faded johnnies and psychedelic pajamas,
in wheelchairs exact as nurses'
steel smiles, they roll, shuffle,
skitter toward the cafeteria's
warm cabbagey embrace.

Whistling, an orderly pushes a basket
down the hall, collecting the clothes
of dreams. As the sunlight fades
a single transistor swells
pumping its narcotic to each heart.

Having confronted certain reassuring nurses
and reassuring uncertain doctors,
having watched their children stagger toward flowers
in the wake of bees or smile at the blur
of gold inching high across their faces

or wheel bright chrome insects
down a carefully trimmed green path,
parents murmur once more toward the parking lot.
Doors slam. A dim blue vacuum sucks
each car away from a listening room.

Above the great boxes of shadow
innocent as a sleeping factory,
the stars burn cold and white as faces
preserved in ether. The flowering thorn
folds upon itself and dreams toward dawn.

The Moose on Ledyard Bridge

This wandering bull moose caused a big stir in Hanover, Norwich, and West Lebanon Saturday. The mature moose was first spotted in Norwich, crossed the Ledyard bridge into Hanover and disappeared . . . heading for the West Lebanon line.
—*Valley News* photo caption

Cars snap points of light
against the sun. Patiently he waits
between the scrub birch and pine. Soon
all dies to a distant whirr. Huge bones
slowly lean into each other and the moose
scuffs and waltzes down the sandy cut,
measures his large splayed hoofs along
the sticky tar. The bridge is clear
and on the other side floating in a muff
of heat black needles knit
a sleeve up the shoulder of Moose
Mountain.

      Crossing the bridge
he looks over the rail and watches his long
bearded muzzle sprout from the deep mud
and float away again and again. It is
the river god—the great forked horns
supplicate like trees, tug at the sky
like paws, twist and bleed away,
returning with the returning ripple. His
dribbling beard maps the valley spreading
to the sea. Turning his head he
ambles the last fifty yards, apparently not
noticing the squealing Buick skid a little

to its side, the camera-flash reflect
in his unblinking eyes.

Over Moose Mountain
the sky is polished blue, the red tower-light
bleached by the sun. Stones lean together
like the bones of mammoths. Something
in a stifling hollow where
last year's leaves are faded puce
rises in a small whirlwind of dust and
listens as it has listened for two-hundred
years to farmers hunting their sheep, hikers
from the college, picnickers, lovers—
always behind a screen of trees. Something rises
and draws in the dead air through a mossy
mask. The cries of half-starved Indians
fade down the slope, arrows sprout from its
side and slip backwards through the trees.
It inhales the long swamp of a cry
and breathes it again, silent, across
eight miles.

Its future, lounging on the New Hampshire
side of the bridge, overlooking a reporter,
ceases chewing his cud. All legs stiffen
and he bolts into the woods past the Canoe Club,
antlers wreaking antlers from the trees.
Trailing leaves drunkenly, he
breaks up Wheelock St. avoiding
the small rocks of Volkswagens, is last seen
puncturing the junk-festooned wilderness of
Mink Brook winding among Model-T's
through whose broken windshields
nose the silver ghosts of trout, finally
reels up the true stream after

the cry of his ancestor waiting
in a tiny storm of leaves.

The last sun soaks like blood into the hill-
side. Panting, legs strain upward, a moving tree
bobbles, disappears among fixed saplings, clangs
against the rust-streaked leg of the relay tower,
quivers to a halt.

                        Then
the answering cry, hoarded in the genes for
two-hundred years, nursed in the gray swamps,
hurled in the scissoring teeth of wolves,
against the red-checked shirts opening
little lights at a distance, smashed against
the yellow diesel's maddening steel horn:
That cry unheard by the men of Hanover—that cry
rooting in the cracks of rocks, knitting
the trees over the bald shoulders of
mountains, driving the trout like leaves,
drawing the hills into the circle of its secret—
winds into the valley with the sun's thickening blood,
covers everything not listening like night.

Gettysburg: The Wheatfield

for
Lee & John Fink

The wheat is swimming toward the sun
in the utter gale of Pennsylvania,
picking the light of stones and pushing
cataracts of trees over the hills.
I see the spotless blue sky swept
clean by the hurrying fields, think of
beards matted with sweat and pollen,
oozing cherry, sour apple, hoarse cries—
the bee dizzily searching for the smashed hive.

"I heard a buzzing sound that stopped.
He took another step and kind of withered.
Funny how he took that step—his hand
went up as if to brush away a fly."

I hear only what I've read
in *American Heritage,* the centennial histories,
voices that scrawl over the years
like the blue smoke from wood-lots,
or drop with loose-jointed ease
like chips from an axe before the furious
tree pulls the sky on the clearing;
and see what I have brought to see,
slickly embalmed from the Brady photos,
to frame with empty trees and fences—
officers baggy around a tilting table,
men leaning against the hind-end of a howitzer,
or twisted in the grass, mouths cocked open,
ravenous for flies.

Yet all of this seems hardly plausible
among the dusty grass continually scratching
itself. The creases in my tourist map have
worn through several strategic positions.

11

In my car again, driving west,
I think of the druids,
whose wicker victims whistled through the fire—
how each year the yellow harvest
climbed wave after wave upon the burning
until, the granaries full, the chieftains fat,
the site was cleaned up for the tourists.
At Auschwitz one reads with mild surprise
the oven-manufacturer's name
stamped on his ware—the baker's hands are
immaculate, white with flour. For a moment
the sun stops. The West swells
around the clot, seeps
through trees . . .

For two weeks afterward at night
you could see the manes of fires
riding over the treetops, splitting
the horses' teeth, melting their hooves,
until wet with the dawn their clean ribcages,
curved like the hulls of decaying arks,
floated empty over the fields.

Bloody Angle, 1964

The grass is copper-green in the storm's
preliminary flash. With lantern cheeks
they come swaying over the swaying
grass and trees. They come steadily

as the middle dark of the storm blotting
the landscape, faces no one can focus
upon, thin afterthoughts of smoke,
burlap shredding to weeds.

Trees split at the touch
of a bright blue blade. Their eyes
hiss in all directions like the rain.
Hills bucket the sound. Suddenly

they're on us! Everything slurs,
thrashes to its root,
flashing upward with the branches.
We feel them pass in cold shoals,

pockets of air light with purpose.
Our skin tightens to a drum as rank
upon rank establish both horizons,
cold fish moving underseas

eyeless and easy, casting a slight
fluorescence. The wind's long
breathless chain of seed
rattles from the far hills

skelters through the opposed
myriad trees and fences.
The vacuum of their going
closes hard upon the mailed waters.

Our pores at attention, light signals
the cloud's retreat. Each grass grows still,
holding its bright bead of battle. A thrush
unstops his buried hoard of breath.

Two

Poet

Found out in left hayfield
under a crooked moon
bought in a green bottle
in a back alley in Wales
plucked from a rock
where the sea goes rabid—
at night the pink feet
wizen to little hooves.

The transparent extra lid
the elastic web hidden
between silken fingers
in a red wool mitten
or the nibbed horn buried
in a field wild with curls—
may be trimmed at six
burned away like a wart.

Though his violet irises
be put under glass
in a symmetrical frame
arranged for at school—
dangerous in adolescence
liable under the moon
to be changed to an elm
married to tulips.

Holds the earth like a marble
between finger and thumb
breathes through grasses
belches clouds
sprouts words like pimples
hoards his shame
evokes a sly lip
from a name.

Grown glues his feet
under the stars
holds his mind inside out
like a Klein jar
up to the world maybe—
maybe not—
his clothes hung about him
like an afterthought.

Grandfather Chance

Farming the yellow squares he learned a rage
for wheat like the sun stooping red-faced over the
     field,
for hogs anchoring a cloud of dust by the trough,

barns fat with summer, a tractor's shining cleats,
and lilacs muffling the house in a burning cloud.
He learned his way about land, machinery, men,

tilled, repaired, talked, bought and sold
early and late, then drove his Plymouth off the road
when work rose up to take its share of him.

Two heart attacks later I knew his easy walk
across the porch where the screen door yawned
as it swung wide on the cindered street:

his retired black shoes made a comfortable squeak
as if the earth liked his weight upon it.
Outside the ice cream parlor yellow hats

stirred the moist air. Cold orangeade sweated
as, clearing the gravel from his throat, he paused
listening to the whine of the single cooler.

Mornings he'd take me early to fish
for the green catfish I played with on the bank,
trapping in pools till the little dykes gave way—

or ignored entirely to hurt him with my book,
asserting my independence. When he died,
swinging a tailgate shut behind some new calves,

I recalled the way his dentures clicked
cracking strawberry seeds, the morning light
flooding the cantaloupe he cut for me in cubes.

Miss Foster

I see the schoolbus let them off at school
like some brightly colored mechanical sow
casting her litter patiently under the trees

or Noah's Ark on wheels. Free, they run
scuffing a white glitter from the grass,
their voices a thinning circle of sharp sound.

Noon stretches out on the enameled hull.
Leaves swim thin and dusty in the light
blazing like Lucifer on the windshield.

Wheeling to the cool side of the porch
where aphids' milk leaves the railing tacky,
I sleep with locusts singing in the garden.

Later, as the sun narrows to a coal
floating in each of the bus's seven windows,
their laughter snags me like the shriek of chalk.

In twos and threes they whisper past my house
to clatter up the iron-stippled stair
as darkness floods the world. With a small sigh

steel doors swallow the last pair.

Mad Dog   That night the dog let night in
Moonlight bubbled down his chin

Spilling across the porch. Thoughtful, he
Tore the black grass, sniffed what he'd torn,

Bayed a silk slip weeping from a line.
We could not get to him in time

Nor out of it—two pearls, his eyes
Crabbed sideways in the tide.

Purring, a car crouched two houses down,
Its blue eye sifting, sifting through the trees.

Shapes sidled up, a low voice hung
Its noose about his head. Snarling, he
Kinked into the street. A shot—

He took the moon at a lope. We heard
His bark drift back like distant stars
A thousand years beyond their fires.

Reflection

*for Kenneth &
Liese Shewmaker*

Our boat floats on a drifting cloud of men—
their poles crinkle jaggedly like lightning,
their faces blend with sky and long arms
crook, fingers on the water fleeting.
I lift our net and watch the nylon weep
haloes receding outward from each drop.

The Catch

The floating world reveals itself
briefly under the lake's
sliding top—the rivering weeds, the sudden
stick of a cruising pike, the convoluting
clouds behind the image of my face
shaking over quicksilver waters
and by the shore where trees lurk
millennia deep in the bright shallows,
sleep-watching as waves undo their leaves
spring summer fall summer spring
and snail eggs ride up the pier.

From the cabin a rich pulse
of light beats across the water
now black as glass, fire unfolding
from a kerosene lamp memories of the red eye
that opened and closed hissing on a stone
while curled with my grandfather, half-asleep,
I dreamt the single story of the woods
in all its variations: the blue feathered
cruelty of winter, light
loopholing the April leaves,
the watchful drowse of summer smoking with flies.

We lift our catch: they shudder in the dark
and thump against the ribcage of the pier
as mosquitoes redouble the attack.
We shove through the cabin door: a mixed smell
of varnish, cedar, lamp, catches our breath. There
links of moonlight swinging from our fists
open and close their gills for the lake
that shook this moment from its silver mesh.

A Bear

for
Judson and
Shirley Scruton

A white bear groped the orchard of my dream,
Gulped cherries down his inexact raw throat,
His paws were bleeding blindly and his muzzle,
Sweet cherry, sweet cherry, sweet cherry—

                                          I shot
The huge blind bear so enormously stuffing
Himself with winds of flowers, heaps of grass-
Green partridges, red and yellow marmosets,

And down he came with the bread of heaven
Thunderous on my brazen coat. I deferred
Handshakes and all grave bear solemnities,
Touching his wounded eyes and ears and nose.

He sang a slow song as he smoothly died,
Lifting his nose to the east and to the west,
A thin and quavering note for so large a beast
That crept in a slow stain across my vest.

Then blazing like a furnace of white snow
He lifted cavernous wings and drew
To his full height—his blood hung in bright beads—
He flexed his feathers once and flew

In a flattering arc to the sun that swelled
Imperceptibly to drink him in, then shone
As usual. Each day it's shone the same
Since I first rubbed my eyes to find him gone.

24

Three

Snakesong

In the green swim of trees

in the silk clothes of spring

when sparse birds

made a singing net

and small red barks

split at the green nudge

I clung to the trunks

went under the roots

to the heart of the pull

sidled, rustled

sloughed off my skin

and waved my word

thin red fire

around the spotted

and dewed damps of life

small numps

uncurling

twigs ticking and swelling

flames of newts

rabbits in scuds

puffing like milkweed.

I curled round the garden

thin hose of breath

noose of the spirit

simple string

undone by everything.

Such I was

before I walked a man

or made palaver

or wavered at woman

before that sweet fig

fixed my tooth

and, scotched, I sagged

to the cellar of roots

and coiling thought

soon with feet and hands

to cling to the sky

move upright as a tree

in the crooked light

find my tongue and spread

a mist over the world.

The Way I Hear It

Giving her mother a peck she picked
up the basket loaded with Girl Scout cookies,
zipped up her windbreaker to the hood and started
    down
that path winding so prettily from her house.

Chainsmoking in the wood he waited, his butts
littering the ground like snowdrops. It was,
he reflected, hard to be a wolf, with soft
nails and teeth no longer than the ordinary—

cold, baying at the moon fleeced white as snow,
running with that pack of shadows. He never could
explain the torn knees and elbows to his folks.
He put on his rubber Wolf Man's mask:

"Oh, cut it out, George!" she said, before
he could get out even an ordinary, slightly muted
growl. His claws hung long and pulpy at his side.
"I'll have to," he sighed, "work through Grandma!"

Grandma was tempted until she found
out he meant business, fled screaming to lock
herself in the bathroom and screw
her eye to the keyhole.

In bed, his moustache bristling over the coverlet,
he looked just like her: "Wow, Grandma, what a
heavy upper lip you have! Try the vanilla!" and Hood
was off to a forest ranger in the vicinity

before she could hear his long rehearsed *Thebetter
totickleyouwithmydear!* Grandma squealed.
Skinned and hung up to dry he weighed 137
pounds, which is more than any other wolf

the ranger shot that season. They all noticed
his toes, short and stubby, the absence of a tail,
and called the papers. WOLF BOY! the papers screamed.
"Fifty-third nearly extinct species!"

the Sierra Club warned, but nobody listened,
except, perhaps, Red Riding Hood
who drifting along the sidewalk now hummed
a little, examining in a mirror white teeth, red lips.

The Hunt

*for Rusty &
Charlie Miller*

She never was sure. It might have been
the poplar turning in the garden, that sly
swell of white seeming to look at her,
leaves lifting idly as fingers.
She spoke and a great commotion stirred.
He of the dark beard fixed her eyes.
His head parted slowly: "A unicorn!"

Trumpets bled with the flying sun,
steel hoofs flattened the little leaves,
helmets rocked between the trunks,
and birds continually kept shrieking.
At night fires shook the ground
and the gray twisted necks of the oak
as all simmered to a gutteral snore.

A little water, and she was placed
under the great flowering tree
green with moss from its knees to its shoulders.
A finch bobbled, red eye in the vegetable hair,
flew out. Praying mantises,
archers flexed green bones and waited
for the sun to draw all in a bullseye.

She saw a primrose nod to the ground,
the small flare of a silver hoof,
a forelock of moonlight lost in the day.
One eye held the sea, the other the sky
as the long horn pierced her with music
burning along her arm, the head
floating a thistle to her lap.

                    She couldn't
speak, saw the arrows bloom upside-down
poppies in his haunch. No sound or motion

but the faintest quivering. Then that last
look, and she knew why and
all the yelping horns in the madness
of the noon made no difference,
nor dogs drowning in his broken side.

'B' Movie

Eyes glowing like headlights
    move through the trees
poking holes in darkness
    in search of you and me.

Where shall we hide?   The last plane
    succumbs to black vines, its tires
eaten by ants. We send a radio message
    and the static snickers.

Clutching a little column of noon
    surrounded by spanish moss
we shiver in the violence of our sweat:
    flesh squeaks against flesh.

"Darling," I say to my shadow in your eye
    and point to the sawtooth mountains
where we may just escape the light
    that burns like acid.

The sun falls, a murdered grape.
    We hear only our echoes
gallop through the canyon,
    then far below

a dim signal
    followed by another.
A cluster of insane stars, they close
    swaying sensitive apparatus . . .

We wake where robot faces
    lean in a circle above,
choosing surgical instruments.
    I ease out of one sleeve

and lunge at the lasar eye—
    glass—blue sparks—metal groans—
then grab you and crawl through smoke.
    Incredibly, help comes.

Later, where the moon foams like lather
    on the wet cheek of the sand,
we two, new-pressed, clean-shaven,
    clinch . . . fade out . . . THE END.

Nude

Content in her skin she does not challenge
the blue shadow cast over most of her body,
waiting in the shade like a center of gravity,
so full, even the trees have travelled too far.

Her breasts steal the wind with surprise,
promise long savannahs of discovery
beyond the trembling compass of a flower
or tuft of weeds agog with her sweet breath.

I stand in this museum looking,
blood sagging to my fingers and toes.
The sun is coming at me through the wall.
Clothes could never touch her, this one, put
beyond the night whisper and morning's flat red
    mouth
into the first turning of the light.

At the Edge

for Roberta

The field is smoking gold

with ragweed, Blackeyed Susan,

and the sun gathering itself from the grass.

At the edge one tree

harps on the end of summer.

A faint buzzing of light about your navel,

the sands are white and tremble to my cheek.

In the canyon tumbleweed hides moisture.

All day our eyes

powdered by the blue mothwing

stitched round with moving swords of grass—

this sky,

its orange spot

thickening to red.

Your voice an undersong:

water easing the limestone,

the cricket's thin leg

    against a bowl of sky,

        the world humming on its axle

full with sleep.

The Chair

for FWS

Here you sat as a sense of dark peace
moved through our house with the aroma
of your cigaret and held the rafters up.

Outside the night breathed with tires
passing in the rain. One streetlight fixed
its spoke in the world. From my bed

I imagined your face in repose over the page
as still your hand stirred and knocked
ash off the glowing eye. All

the dark rooms were comfortable and true.
I felt the lamp reach up the stair
from where you kept the house

in a slow circle about the sun
and the long sigh of the iron
smoothed tomorrow.

Now in my own house I sit in the same chair
in the same long channel of time
and feel the fathers each riding

the sure nights of peace,
though rafters blow like leaves
and lights slip from the world.

Four

Hunting in Widener Library

Ribithoids, by Macrowcz, 073.869.10-6A, written on a
slip of paper floating between fingers before him
to the narrow door, hedged in stone,
the same stone shelving out over,
under, eons of books compressed into
ten levels, wedged in steel vertebrae,
ganglia for the enormous brain that sheds
a little light out these windows—once
John Harvard's few shelves, now plunging
stories into the earth.

                                                    Going down
from Level 4 to Level 3, from American
to English literature, oppressed
by the millions of cells thinking
in the darkness between covers,
the word buried in the pulp of trees.
Down to Sub-level B. Stairs clang: up the
square mouth a soft meadowy thing in a sweater,
books pressed quivering to her, cloud
of flowers, momentary. Then that staid
smell of old authors shrinking in the cellar,
distant seed of the tree of knowledge
more elusive for its sextillion sprouts,
steady and shrewd scent of worlds
never to be cracked. Down
to Sub-level D. The slip is pale
against the blue fluorescent damp—
potable stone.

Ribithoids, by Macrowcz, an unintelligible title
by an unpronounceable author—reason enough:
This is the book to break that
chain of looking up to add
to what one knows, which always leads to

looking up something else. Bald-headed man asleep on
the second, third, and eighth volumes
of Crabbits' *Dictionary of the Visigoths.* The
radiator clucks like a brooding hen.

This is the book to give the secret
whole—the isolate knowledge, ethereal
and complete, in whose faintest iota swims
the luminous gnat-swarm of the worlds.
This is the fruit whose pierced skin
froths with stars, at whose succulent word
the snake swallows his tail into light.
This is the fruit of that forbidden tree
whose roots crawl over maps and faces,
sink through this cellar nine
times all of relative space to the center.

He moves along the last aisle, bulb burnt out,
lighting a match over the backward books—
Ribwort, Ribs—then nothing but solid
wall one inch away from Macrowcz 10-6A
buried in stone!

The snake's skeleton rattles through the pipes.
The gleaming-headed sleeper after knowledge
snores. Back to Coleridge and Lowes'
Road to Xanadu, where he who pauses to pluck
a footnote is lost. Back to the link
that is not missing, back to Coleridge and
opium, the regulated stall, books
to check in and books to check out.

The root goes too deep.

In a Farmhouse Near Porlock

for
Robert Barth

*"In the summer of the year 1797, the author,
then in ill health, had retired to a lonely
farmhouse between Porlock and Linton . . ."*
—Coleridge's Introduction to "Kubla Khan"

At home in her kitchen wife Sara grieves:
The tiles are unmended, the shoe money gone.
When she poured boiling milk on that abstracted form,
It had smiled and written a three-shilling poem.*

In a farmhouse near Porlock Coleridge sleeps
As the red moon licks itself to a ball.
A Collector from Porlock knocks loud through the hall:
Is anyone here, anybody at all?

By a farmhouse near Porlock a frayed moon sings
Like the bitter half of a wedding ring.
Huge blocks of night beat on the wall
And a tree shakes the green pulse of a star:
Nobody here, nobody at all!

In a farmhouse near Porlock sun and moon walk
Like red and silvery crabs on the sand,
Cold hand in hot where the heavens crack white,
And a head splits wide at the edge of a voice:
Is anyone, anyone here at all?

And there in the midst of the whirligig
Light put its stick and broke the string,
Night hooted by on its rickety rails,
The garden sprung, the day shook free,

All space snaked by and a mind floated blithe
As a bubble on a column of breath,
The lion rolled out his red-carpeted tongue,
Lambs leaped in the green fields of his breath.

45

Then the fist fell like a cindered star.
The door licked dry lips, the lid snapped down.
A Man a Man a Man from the Town!—
A shoestring was broken, the fire out—
"Here I am! Lord! Here I am!"
And Coleridge went out.

* An earlier poem, "This Lime-Tree Bower My
Prison," written after the recounted accident
prevented Coleridge from going on a walk with
the Wordsworths and Lamb.

Leaves of Grass
(1860)

God bless Thayer & Eldridge who
published *Leaves of Grass*, going
bankrupt the very next year. They wrote:

"Dear Walt,

                                       We
read the book with profit and pleasure,
want to publish a true poem and writ
by a *true* man. We
have great facilities and numberless
Agents (we do not 'puff' here but
speak *truth*). We are young men. We
celebrate ourselves by acts. Try us.
You can do us good, we can
do you good *pecuniarily*."

                                   They stand
one with his thumbs aimed around gray galluses
the other with his beaver tilting the sky
in a Boston street where soot is negligible.

Inside, their soon-to-be auctioned press
grins with level teeth
black grease glistening on its wheels.
Some Upper Case slum with lower case:
It is Boston, 1860.

Walt bless Thayer & Eldridge who
standing in a yellow light did no one,
were done no, pecuniary good.

Leaves of grass grow under their feet
sprout from their pockets
(sun making it through whatever soot)
muffling those great facilities, numberless agents,

wrapping around their arms and faltering thumbs.

They read the book finally with no profit:

Flowers graze their lips.

March Moon

for
Helen de Vette

The moon hangs like a face
waiting for a returning look
to take no features but my own
as it swims silently with the car
through this crevice in the earth.

A barn mounted like a stone
keeps the secret of life—
an underground rumor that shakes
this perfect white field of snow
quivering blue in the light.

A brook pioneers a culvert,
its soft tooth gnawing the ice,
shaking the dream of the sleeper,
a white sloth who has over-stayed,
whose breath has fanged all the trees.

The stars blink wider and warm
conspiring with mole and worm
who deep in a stupor now stir
uncoiling with roots of flowers
to give the sun back to the sun.

The cloud of my breath on the glass
where the moon hangs in a halo
hurries away from the fan.
Sharp eyes, mouth, one-sided nose
stare back through the whistling air.

The Cow

The cow's tongue simplifies the grass.
A cloud, whiter than a sword, flicks at her tail
swinging its censer over the trees.
Her holy foot casts out the pail

like a broken god. Behind the barn
electric clouds lure from the trees
that bald sheen of El Greco's that immures
within a cheekbone heavenly infantries

as if all things are foil packaging
instant apocalypse. I see
the moment by this light and poke
El Greco's grass and sky. A sweet

yearning sound breaks open the world:
A bluer sky is there and shining sword.
Miles thick and only an inch away
the cow burns like an angel of the Lord.

The Rock

Stars enough to break a net
And you could smell the new shoots
Groping after them. No moon:
That was my only hope.

After the other left we knew
Something was up. He led us
By that strange parting look
Through night thick with trees.

We drifted in and out of sleep.
He kept coming around, silently
Accusing us it seemed. "Lie down,"
We murmured, "Lie down!"

"Lie down?"—he laughed a little,
His shadow across the stars.
Occasionally a noise in the bushes
Tickled our fears.

I must have dozed off. Suddenly
Sleep in my eyes and fire,
Hooded shapes drawn up,
Then a flat voice: "He's ours."

Reflex!—his weary words—
The angry murmur of flames.
I tried to stay near . . . I wanted to see . . .
(Someone was taking down names)

But tripped over my northern tongue—
I . . . I . . . not I!—
When that meddlesome bird
Broke open the bloody sky.

The Journey

*for
Erwin Rudolph
Sr. and Jr.*

That journey took us along rivers draining in black
    swamps
up cliffs of rotting purple stone
through cities where each whisper startled its ghost

to castles where white weeds
scraped and hissed in the dungeons
and dust writhed at the top of the stairs

across oceans whose monotonous wrinkles
drove the crew mad, whose horrors
spawned under a bladdery sun.

When the weather turned we were sorry
begrudging our skins their returning color.
Our minds at first refused the simple air

the green hill's poisonous innocence
and cliffs white as flowers the waves bore to them.
Restlessly we paced the lean-cheeked ship.

One morning we woke later than usual
none having kept watch. The air was rich
with those things we'd denied our hearts

compressed by disaster. Trees broke
the horizon quiet and sharp. There was a shining
among the trunks: Some heard singing. Then . . .

words fail like the chaffing of landward gulls!

A
Hilly
River
Landscape

for
Dain & Vera
Trafton

That cow in Aelbert Cuyp's river landscape
is sitting in the center and she knows it.
Activity, human, equine, around her
moves in a circle shifting with the clouds.

A rider leads his horse into the river,
another curbs his sharply to the shore,
a third spurs his toward where the first is drinking.

In the foreground two dogs curl in doggy play.
Their master, redcoated, aloft on his horse,
points with his crop toward a violet horizon
while a shepherdess waits wooden for command.

Whatever is out there, they'll move toward it
with those grand stageprops of staff and whip.
But the cow is already there, glowing dull copper,
her four stomachs sorting the dreams of the world
from the long grasses of the endless pampas.

Five

Morning After the Apocalypse

1.
Turnpike, Exit 44

The moon injects this festering dream into
my passengers' porous sleep—who stir like hills.
Wry ghosts, the signs swell up and whisper by.
Meanwhile on the radio's narrow lip
glows the white coal of revelation.

2.
Air
Field

All day the great planes gingerly descend
an invisible staircase, holding up
their skirts and dignity like great ladies
in technicolor histories, or reascend,
their noses needling upward like a compass
into a wild blue vacuum,
leaving everything in confusion behind:

In some such self-deceiving light as this
we'll view the air force base when moved away
from where its sleepless eye revolves all night.
We'll smile and recollect it conversationally—
tell with what ease the silver planes dropped down
or how they, weightless, rose above
our roof. We'll pass it with the sugar and cream,

forever sheltered from this moment's sick
surprise that we have lived with terror, with pride,
the wounded god circling the globe, never resting,
that in the morning and the evening we have heard
his cry, have seen him drag his silver wings
whining with anguish like a huge
fly seeking to lay its deadly eggs.

**3.
Laodicea,
New
Hampshire**

There is a slow time
between the ridges of these blue New Hampshire hills
in January when cold brings a truce
to all of nature and the snow
locks in a sheet the unjust and the just.

Under a dim blue lens of ice
the trout feel the old
promise of the rock to still be rock.
The trout are very still and then,
as if the earth's teeth snapped, ice

breaks and trickles once more to the sea.
In their new freedom trout dart
streaks of mercury to devour
the sag-mouthed dace and hatching flies
among the cans and sodden shoes.

Under a pale sun rich waters froth
quarter-moons of suds that gleam
through the black needles and the rap
of bulldozers warming in the cold

to cut a road to summer through the rock.

4.
Love Story:
The Sixties

"You can put the tray over there—why
do they have to serve this awful green jello? —
I almost forgot to tell you how Allen and I
originally got together. It's out of sight!
No salt, thanks—rots your teeth—the doctor
cut me down: I was putting on too much weight,
not that it matters now. Yet I can't
stop pampering myself. God, how I wish
this stuff wouldn't shake every time you touch it!

"A year ago I read an ad in the *Crime:*
'Wanted, pregnant Cliffie to help Harvard
junior avoid draft. Marriage will be
strictly *pro forma.* Divorce guaranteed
within two years.' 'Some joke!' I thought. I wasn't
pregnant then, of course, but just for kicks
I answered the ad and there was Allen,
a little nervous about the draft but primarily
curious what sort of person would respond.
I let him think I *was* pregnant, that some
god had walked out of my life. That got to him.
We spent the nights we weren't booking hard
in each other's room. I was careful. *He*
wasn't, of course, thinking I was on my way
anyway. The sex was good. It was
natural. We were very sure about that,
were soon talking tentatively about marriage
and moved in together. I told my parents, who
took it calmly enough but acted ridiculously
uptight the time or two they stopped to see us.

"Allen was relieved when he found out I wasn't
pregnant. We spent most of his senior year
in a miserable efficiency where the bed
fell out of the wall like an ironing board.
Then, for some reason, I *was.* When I told him

60

he didn't even look up from his book, said
I was putting him on and besides it didn't help
with the draft anymore. He began staying
late at the library, which was a relief
because he wouldn't talk to me. Sex was like
stuffing the toaster in the morning.
I no longer answered the letters from home:
We were my folks. Sometimes we smoked a little
grass together and then
we *felt* close—or at least we didn't feel
not-close, or we didn't care.

                 "Just as I
was getting bitchy and possessive Allen
gave up his senior thesis, disappeared.
I nearly went out of my mind! Well, he came back
to make a new start, he said, though something
was obviously wrong. He seemed *too* happy,
stopped going to class and failed his exams.
I guess I knew all the time he was freaking out,
acid, speed, anything. Well, I didn't *care*
by this time—had to think of myself and the baby,
fat mama cat! Allen withered from the scene.
When the call came from the hospital I couldn't
recall for a moment if I knew someone named Allen.
But once I went down it hit me: He was
calm, but not really there, just smiled
and talked about pulling his head together.
The doctor nodded, said he might in time.
I took a room at Radcliffe.

"I told my parents I needed the trip to New York
to research an urban studies paper. (Not too
far off at that!). Nothing hurt. I felt
myself again and, in a funny way, clean.
'One less bomb in the population explosion,'

I thought and still think that. My folks
have never found out, are relieved I'm not
seeing Allen any more. So am I. I spotted him
once near the Square—at a distance, luckily
before he saw me. I can't eat this other
roll—would you like it?"

5.
Fun City

whatever we now believe necessary
to vocalize by phone will
then as soon as we think of it
immediately communicate

BZZZ This is a recording:

we will sing through an electronic choir
that would baffle the seraphim
meanwhile in each office memo boards
will relay every effect at intervals

I am sorry but the number

and the general intermaster
will relate on pre-established templates
the coded responses inclusive without fail
of every variable exponentially considered

you have dialed is no longer

and the minute electric filaments
connecting every home and every brain
through the miniputer inserted at birth
between the skull and pineal gland

in service. Will you please

light instantaneously and unite
in one vast grid of intervolved
opinion and consideration of taste
the least whim of reservation about

hang up and try again. This

the slightest readjustment necessary
to the entirely electronic government
operating interdependently and fusing
each unitary cell in its complectic brain

is a recording: I am (CLICK)

6.
Voice of
Many Waters

for Clyde Kilby

To him that overcometh will I give to eat of the
hidden manna,
and will give him a white stone, and in the stone a
new name
written, which no man knoweth saving he that
receiveth it.

The night is cluttered with stars.
    The drift of the earth
is dark, enormous
    bulking shoulder of the undersea whale
in the Atlantic's winking canyons.
    Trees wait
for the slow stain of day
    walking now over the water
west of England.

    I put two sticks on the fire
on the ghost of logs
    that fade into the red eye
drawing the circle of my campsite
    about which hang
my all-weather tent, glinting axe
    myself, like planets
inching the swarm of stars.

    Twelve o'clock:
The beast startles first with his foot
    broad as unbearable moon,
his leg the shank of stars
    his mane the black roar of space
turning to the white heart of fire
    in which begin to move
thick and uncertain

the rivery shapes of trees
bending over water
    cradling a platinum light
running to gold
    and pebbles
each speckled with suns
    each turned and lapped by the water.

Green steals over me:
    I am swung in a net of leaves.
Birds wrap me tight in their songs:
    drunk with the trauma of flowers
I am and I hear a voice calling
    within the voices of water.
A shadow brightens the ground.
    A hand darkens all but itself.

Somewhere in the face of the trees
    a large clumsy beast is singing
the brood of pain and music
    played on the stops of the worlds
the flute of starlight and vacuum
    the unending theme of Abyss
and the trees are growing before me
    translating all to flowers.

Now the voice is within a white stone
    round in my hand like water
that speaks one word running through fingers
    to shred in my mouth like the moon.
Outside the sun is rising. Blue,
    the sky is blue
and the far forest neighing.

    I wake in the orange flower of my tent.